Cashing Out!

Insights for getting the most from selling your business –

From a master entrepreneur

New, expanded second edition

Dave Berkus

Published by David Berkus DBA The Berkus Press

For corrections, company/title updates, comments, or any other inquiries, please e-mail DBerkus@berkus.com

Second Printing 2014
10 9 8 7 6 5 4 3 2

ISBN   978-1-105-04078-8

Copyright © 2014 by David W. Berkus. All rights reserved. Printed in the United States of America. No part of this publication may be reproduced or distributed in any form or by any means, or stored in a database or retrieval system, except as permitted under Sections 107 or 108 of the U.S. Copyright Act, without prior written permission of the publisher. This book is printed on acid-free paper.

Material in this book is for educational purposes only. This book is sold with the understanding that neither the author nor the publisher are engaged in rendering legal, accounting, investment, or any other professional service. Neither the publisher nor the author assumes any liability for any errors or omissions, or for how this book or its contents are used or interpreted, or for any consequences resulting directly or indirectly from the use of this book. For legal advice or any other, please consult your personal lawyer or the appropriate professional.

The content within this book has been previously published within the books, BASIC BERKONOMICS, BERKONOMICS, and ADVANCED BERKONOMICS. Individual insights from this book are published periodically in Dave's emails and blog, www.berkonomics.com.

Groups may order copies of the book at a group discount by contacting Dave Berkus at 626-355-5375, or at dberkus@berkus.com .

Throughout this book, the Cambria type font was used for headlines, and text was set using the Calibri font.

The views expressed by the individuals in this book do not necessarily reflect the views shared by the companies they are employed by (or the companies mentioned in) this book. The employment status and affiliations of author with the companies referenced are subject to change.

Contents

INTRODUCTION 5

Think of your exit as you commit your resources along the way. 8

Envision the end game. Advance toward the goal. 9

There are three kinds of business buyers. 10

List ten companies that could buy your business. 12

Timing is everything in a sale. 13

Look for your strategic buyer first. 15

Nothing commands a higher multiple than hope! 17

Exit timing and price depends on many factors. 18

Timing your exit – Don't ride it over the top. 19

A successful exit is a great measure of a good journey. 21

Create stakeholder loyalty when times are good. 22

Everyone wants to leave a legacy. 23

Do you engage an investment banker? 24

Start a deal room and keep it current. 26

Leave something on the table in a sale. 27

Money is not the only measure of success. 29

The most satisfying life journey is never about the money. 30

Don't be greedy even if you have the power. 31

Failure is the greatest of teachers. 33

A million things can kill the deal. 34

Share your liquidity success with those who got you there.................. 35

Turning out the lights is a type of exit. 36

My story and what I learned from losing it all. 37

Profit from the lessons learned from total loss. 40

Sell when growth is high, even if cash flow is low. 42

Solve partnership issues before the company sale. 43

Don't be greedy even if you can. 45

The muted thrill of the deal closing. 47

Take the time to celebrate your exit. 48

Entrepreneurs do not easily retire. 50

About the author... .... ***52***

Other books by Dave Berkus available directly from *www.berkus.com* or from your favorite bookseller or online store: 54

INTRODUCTION

This book is the eighth and last in a series of short, easy to read books that guide an entrepreneur through the stages of creation, management, growth, and ultimately sale of a small business enterprise. And this is the second edition of this book, packed with half again as much materials the first edition, published in 2011.

Each section is an insight into another facet of starting a business that is not taught in business school or available in business texts, but rather the result of over fifty years of entrepreneurial experience with my own entrepreneurial companies and serving as investor, coach, mentor and board member for over forty entrepreneurial startups over the years.

Originally published as portions of three books, BASIC BERKONOMICS, BERKONOMCS, and ADVANCED BERKONOMICS, comments from entrepreneurs and professional managers after reading those books led to suggestions that I create separate mini-books for each stage of the business, to appeal to the interests of those at that stage of development, ready to absorb and implement insights that apply directly to the current stage of their business. Make them inexpensive and available as eBooks, they suggested, so that entire teams of managers could use the book as a planning tool and discussion prompt for the team in meetings.

And so this series of Small Business Success Books was born to address an opportunity. You can pick up this book and immediately relate to the insights, issues, opportunities, and exercises in this book right at the earliest stages of creating your business. This is not a replacement for "how to" books, courses, and consultants. It is a deeper opportunity to evaluate, plan, and execute strategies for growth based upon these insights that augment and amplify the usual "how to" materials available to entrepreneurs.

In this book, I'll tell personal stories from my fifty-plus years of entrepreneurial experience. But every one of us has a story to add to this mix, one of passionate entrepreneurism, sometimes inside an existing larger corporation, sometimes alone on a kitchen table, or back room desk. And it is a sure thing that many of us will have cogent, insightful additions to this caldron, culled from their own experiences. There's a place for these in the blog, www.berkonomics.com, and I welcome any and all for others to read and learn.

Dave Berkus

Arcadia, California

P.S. This is the sixteenth publication from *The Berkus Press*. I am very fortunate to have expert help this time from some very smart friends in the business, each of whom has volunteered to contribute one or more insights for this book, directly from their personal experience of working as an entrepreneur or with entrepreneurs. Here's a special thanks to these friends, whose contributions are definitely for your benefit. Whenever one of these excellent insights appear in this book, the first time each contributor's work appears, I'll insert a very short bio for that expert right below the headline. And as always, if no attribution appears for an insight, I'm its author - and to be blamed for any and all errors in judgment and accuracy.

Dave Berkus

Arcadia, California

Cashing Out!

If you took funding from outside investors to make your company a success, you made a pact to build the company in value and someday find a buyer for the business. Professional investors look closely at the entrepreneurs they finance, expecting to find sincerity in that promise. Many serial entrepreneurs hunger for the next opportunity to create a new business, with the rush that comes from the ignition and growth being their greatest reward.

There are many things you and your investors and managers can do to assure a greater likelihood of success in the ultimate sale of the company. And there certainly are effects upon you and others to consider during and after the sale.

This book delves into these issues with a number of insights gained from tens of liquidity events over the years, and of their aftermaths for the various entrepreneurs involved.

Think of your exit as you commit your resources along the way.

Each decision you make to commit resources affects the future value of the business to some degree. Minor decisions, such as replacing employees who have left the company or equipment needing updating, are usually considered operational in nature, and unless the business is changing direction, not relevant to this analysis. But each commitment of resources of any substantial size for acquisition of new products, talent, even new companies, changes the value of your enterprise perhaps to a great degree.

Let's analyze the effect of a potential acquisition upon the value of your company. We must assume that you intend to sell the enterprise at some point in the future. There are many reasons a company finds to make an acquisition. New products, new geographic territories, elimination of a competitor, increase in revenues, consolidation savings, new talent, new distribution channels, and more are good reasons for considering an acquisition.

Given these possible goals in making a good acquisition, there is one overarching question that you should consider before making that decision to acquire a company. Know first that statistically, 80% of all acquisitions do not meet the intended objectives of the acquirer, making most all acquisitions risky. The question to study in your board meeting long before making any offer to purchase a candidate business is: "Would this acquisition add significantly to our enterprise value and attractiveness in an eventual sale?"

If the answer is "no", and there are other opportunities for the use of cash that would add value, it would be wise to allocate resources to those opportunities. After all, we are in business usually for the ultimate return we will someday receive from our investment.

Envision the end game. Advance toward the goal.

When we start a business, we are optimistic that we will succeed and dream of riches to follow when the company is sold or even participating in an IPO. Some of us build our businesses to be lifestyle creations, destined to provide for our families but not necessarily as creators of great equity upon an eventual sale. But most of us dream of selling the business someday for lots of money and building our wealth upon that event.

So it is important to envision that end game even at the outset, especially when planning to take in money from others as investors, all of whom will seek a payoff someday in a sale or IPO.

An effective way to do this is to make a list of up to ten possible future buyers of the business, and to spend time defining what those buyers would want when purchasing your business. Would it be your intellectual property? Your skilled employees? Your brand and market recognition? Your distribution channel relationships? Whatever you envision that value to be, you should work to build that portion of your business by paying special attention to it as you work to build the operation.

Step by step as you make decisions to allocate your scarce human and financial resources, you should remember where the ultimate value should be at the end game. It will help you to explain the value of your business to potential investors and certainly help focus your efforts as you advance toward that goal of a liquidity event in your future.

There are three kinds of business buyers.

This is one of my favorite insights, since I lived this one in a positive exit from my computer business. Most people will tell you that there are two kinds of eventual buyers for your business: *financial* and *strategic*. A financial buyer will analyze your numbers, past and forecast, to the n'th degree, and calculate the price based upon the result, after carefully comparing your numbers with those of others in the same and similar industries. The object of a financial purchase is to negotiate a bargain, capable of payoff through operating profits or growth over time, or even of immediate profit from arbitrage – knowing of a purchaser that is willing to pay more for your company if repackaged, or even with no changes at all.

A strategic purchaser is one that understands what your company has to offer in its marketplace, and how your company will add extra value to the purchaser's company. Strategic buyers look for managerial talent, intellectual property, geographic expansion, an extension into adjacent markets and more that will be achieved with the acquisition of your company. Such a purchaser usually is willing to pay more to secure this new leverage, understanding that the value of the acquisition is more than the mere financial value of your enterprise. Most investment bankers will coach you into helping them find you a strategic buyer, knowing that such sales are quicker, often less focused upon the small warts of a business, and yield higher prices than financial sales.

There is a third class of buyer I discovered first hand when selling my company - the *emotional* buyer. This rare buyer *needs* your company. He must have you or one of your competitors, and now. The buyer may be a public company attempting to defend decreasing market share and being overly punished by Wall Street. You may represent the only obvious way to protect against obsolescence from a buyer's declining marketplace, or failure to compete against others with better, newer technologies. You may be a most successful direct competitor, one that the buyer's sales people have observed jealously and nervously, sometimes even jumping over to your company as a result. No matter what the emotional focus, the buyer cannot continue to stand by and watch its business challenged so effectively. The price negotiated is not at all the critical factor in the emotional sale. It is the elimination of pain that drives the buyer to action.

I experienced just this phenomenon and profited by the added value in the transaction provided by an emotional public company buyer for my business. The potential buyer was a hardware company, well aware that margins were decreasing and that software companies, once considered mere vehicles to help sell hardware, were now becoming the central component in a sale, mostly because hardware was fast becoming a commodity as prices dropped. My buyer-candidate had previously licensed our firm as a distributor, a value-added reseller for its hardware. As we grew to capture 16% of the world market in our niche, we successfully migrated from the single platform of the buyer-candidate onto hardware from any of its competitors from IBM to NCR to HP and others. At the same time, the buyer-candidate realized that we had become its largest reseller. In one of many meetings with the buyer's CEO, I "accidentally" dropped the truthful fact that his hardware now accounted for only about a third of our hardware revenues, down from 100% several years earlier. It did not take but moments for him to realize that his largest reseller was giving his company only a third of its business, that his revenues were declining and ours increasing dramatically. Simple in-the-head math shocked him into the realization that, if he could increase our use of his equipment in more sales, that he could slow or stop the decline in his revenues and he could migrate into a more software-centric company, much more highly valued by Wall Street, which was punishing his company for its decline and coming obsolescence.

The resulting negotiation was rather quick and very lucrative for our side. It was the first time I had witnessed an emotional buyer, and appreciated the difference between "strategic" and "emotional" immediately. Ever since, I have been urging my subsequent company CEO's and boards to perform an exercise at regular intervals to seek out and identify future strategic and emotional buyers. We'll describe that exercise in the next insight.

List ten companies that could buy your business.

This is an exercise I perform with my boards no less than once every several years in planning exercises attended by the board and senior management, sometimes augmented with an industry consultant or expert from the outside.

Use a white board visible to the entire group. Draw and label four columns and ten rows. The columns: "Name of candidate buyer", "what they want", "what we want" and "likelihood".

Then in a brainstorming session, fill in the ten rows with the names of ten potential purchasers of the business, looking deeply for strategic and emotional candidates (see insight 91). Next, return to the list on the board and have the group do its best to divine what it is about your company that would most attract the buyer if it had perfect knowledge of your business and its resources. This could be your intellectual property, your geographic reach, your superior product, your management team, or perhaps your dominant position. Next, have the group focus upon column three, ignoring the obvious gain our company would make in liquidity to shareholders. List what the company would most gain in new resources from this acquirer. Would it be more cash for expansion, new intellectual property, better distribution, completion of drug trials, or more? And finally, have the group put a number in column four, estimating the likelihood of such a sale ever being consummated, with "10" the absolute highest and "1" unlikely to occur.

The magic of this exercise is not only in the organization of group focus upon the liquidity event and possible buyers. It is in revisiting column two of the chart. You will quickly note that at least four of the ten candidates, if each had perfect knowledge of your company and its resources, would want the very same thing from an acquisition. Whatever that is, it shines as the true core competency of your corporation, whether previously expressed or even recognized by management. It is in this area where I would redirect resources such as manpower and money, to build value more effectively and quickly than in any other area of the enterprise.

Occasionally, the insight gained from this exercise comes as a complete surprise to the board and management. And that is most rewarding to see.

Timing is everything in a sale.

I have saved this next story until now because it is one of my favorites, and certainly illustrates the point as well as anything I could devise from fiction.

First here is a bit of the background. The year was 1998. After presenting a "state of the company" report at a national meeting of resellers for a company where I sat on the board, I was approached by one of the audience members, complimenting my presentation and stating, "I have a problem. I've been offered $15 million for my company and my partner is suing me for all I am worth. What can I do?" I promised to come see him at his office the very next week. What I discovered was a contradiction that was too intriguing to ignore. The company of eight was engaged in web design, hot at the time. And yes, the partner had a valid suit, having been locked out of the business and denied access to decisions and accounting information. But the real asset became obvious at almost exactly 5 PM that day, when all eight stopped what they were doing and began using a tool they had licensed from a Florida company to find other Internet gamers to join them in playing intense first party shooter games over the 'net. The tool it turns out had been posted on the company's website and downloaded by over a million gamers. Over a million of these came to the company's game web site each month for new information and to form an early Internet game community. The company made little effort to charge for the software or community. Microsoft had just bought Hotmail for $9 per registered user; AOL had just bought ICQ for $40 per registered user. And here were over a million users, with no apparent value to the web designers, except as a community of friends with similar interests.

I did forget to tell you that on that day looking into the company's books I discovered that neither the company nor its founder had filed Federal income tax returns during the three years in business, didn't I? And there were other quite obvious problems, unattended to, along with the partner's suit hanging over their heads.

I immediately agreed to come aboard at no cost to clean up the corporation, deferring my investment until that was done. I negotiated a settlement with the partner for $100 thousand which I paid, then filed all of the overdue tax returns of various types, and cleaned up the books. Offering to reincorporate the game company as a new entity to avoid any more surprises, we negotiated 10% for my $100 thousand, with the remaining 90% for the founder. In addition, I loaned the new company $150 thousand for working capital. By this time there were not one but four million registered users.

Within three months, we easily obtained $3 million of investment at a pre-money valuation of $30 million. Can you begin to tell that this is a story of timing, and of the Internet bubble? Three months later, another investor company in the business offered to invest $3 million at a valuation of $60 million. Two months after that, a French game company offered $1.5 million at a valuation of $80 million. Of course we took all of these.

We now jump forward to February, 2000, 14 months after formation of the company. Another major competitor in the industry, directly competing with one of our investors, offered $140 million for 49% of the company in a combination of equal cash and stock in its public entity.

Fast forward a month to a meeting between a senior executive of the buyer, our hero the entrepreneur, our corporate attorney and myself. In planning for the transition about to take place, the executive stated to the entrepreneur, "You know, we are buying only 49% so that we do not have to roll your losses into our income statement; but we do expect to make the decisions as if a majority owner." Our entrepreneur, engorged with the year's effortless value increases, turned to the executive without a pause, and said something to the effect of "Hell no! We can make this company worth a billion without you!" And so, a mere month before the crash of the Internet bubble, the buyer withdrew the offer. And, even if some of us were more than unhappy, we went back to the work of building the company value. And a month later the bubble burst.

It took almost four years to sell the company for over $60 million, not at all a bad outcome for us founders and the early shareholders. And I do need to note that the entrepreneur in the meantime became a model executive of a growing company, much more mature and understanding of market forces than that fateful day in February, 2000.

Could I have found a better example of "Timing is everything"? The lesson: Look for cycles in your business and in the marketplace. There are natural high points in one or both that may not be obvious until looking back. But they occur often enough to watch for and take advantage of if ready to make the run for a liquidity event.

Look for your strategic buyer first.
By John Huston

John Huston *is founder and manager of the 300+ member Ohio TechAngel Funds and a past Chairman of both the Angel Capital Association and the Angel Resource Institute.*

While you are busy building your high growth venture, you may have occasionally thought about which large companies might be the ultimate buyer of your company – a buyer that could optimize your idea, customer base, and team. If you have professional angels or venture capitalists among your funding sources, you have probably been focused on your company's sale well before they wrote their first checks.

To simplify the obvious question, you should ask: "In whose hands does my company have the greatest value?" But remember that each potential acquirer should be evaluated in terms of both their *ability* and their *willingness* to make an acceptable offer for your company.

Assessing their *ability* is fairly straightforward, especially if you will only take an all-cash bid. You merely need to forecast the likelihood over the next few years they will have the financial resources to be the high bidder for your venture. For publicly traded potential acquirers, reviewing their public filings regarding previous acquisitions can be quite illuminating - especially finding information about whether they have borrowed to finance past company purchases. Many large companies have a preferred template from which their deal teams rarely stray.

Once you are comfortable with a potential acquirer's ability to make a winning bid for your company, then you only need to focus on how to increase their *willingness* to do so. Ideally each target company has a history of consistently making acquisitions with deal terms you would accept. This means they routinely acquire strategic assets and not just financial cash flow streams, paying a premium to do so.

Let's presume that you have identified three to five targeted bidders whose interest in acquiring your company you now need to heighten. How can you accomplish this?

The first step should be to honestly assess the allure your company might have to each targeted strategic acquirer. Then think about how your company's daily activities are enhancing that most attractive aspect of your business in the eyes of each potential bidder. This makes it much easier to allocate your capital as you prepare for a sale of the company - since the goal is to spend it only in ways which will impress just a few companies. Cash spent on activities which do not burnish your attractiveness is cash squandered as you prepare for the sale.

Buyers, especially strategic buyers, pay premiums over book or shareholder value. That premium is your focus. And it can only be truly determined once the buyer's wire transfer appears in your account.

When you were just commencing commercial sales and refining your business model to achieve positive cash flow, you were focusing on survival. Now, the sooner you can allocate your cash and activities toward impressing targeted strategic bidders, the sooner that beautiful wire transfer will arrive in your bank account.

Nothing commands a higher multiple than hope!
By David Steakley

David Steakley, a past President of the Houston Angel Network, is a reformed management consultant. He is an active angel investor, and he manages several angel funds in Texas.

You may recall that earlier in this book, I explained the definition of an inciting incident, using the movie industry and its story telling as the model. The inciting incident in a movie is the event at the beginning of the story that causes the hero's life to be completely transformed and irrevocably changed, and makes the whole story unfold.

I thought of this in a recent liquidity event in one of my portfolio companies. The company provides identity theft protection, and took a large round from a private equity firm, which returned about eight times investment in cash to the early angels, and still left them with all their stock in the deal, an outstanding result. The CEO did an absolutely masterful job in this transaction. The key to this was: *Nothing commands a higher multiple than hope.* The company had done very well, growing revenue rapidly, and demonstrating excellent results in several diverse sales channels. It had refined its offerings to the point where its service was the clear market leader. So with that tail wind behind, let's quickly bring in the freshly minted MBA to calculate the present value of the discounted future cash flows, and cash in!

Not so fast. The company had a number of potentially huge, blockbuster deals in progress. No one could say what these deals could be worth, or even whether they would ever be consummated. But, they were clearly mouthwatering. This prospect was what enabled the company to command a multiple of revenue so high that I first thought it had to be a typo. As we often hear, "You don't sell the steak, you sell the sizzle."

When you're selling your company, you have to work hard on your story, and the story doesn't really begin until the inciting incident.

Exit timing and price depends on many factors.
By Basil Peters

Basil Peters is perhaps the best known name in the world of early stage company exits. His groundbreaking book, "Early Exits" has become a textbook for angel groups and entrepreneurs throughout the world. His Strategic Exits Corporation provides M&A advisory services, and he is much in demand as a speaker at angel and entrepreneur events worldwide.

Selling an entire company is similar to selling shares in the public markets – how much you can get depends on how the company is doing, but also on how the overall market is behaving. For many stocks, the overall market is a bigger factor than how the company is actually doing at any point in time.

This 'external effect' is even more pronounced when an entire company is being sold because the market for companies is much less 'efficient.'

At the end of 2008, near the bottom of the debt bubble collapse, the overall stock market had dropped about 50%. If there was a similar index for the value of entire companies being sold, I am sure it would have gone down much farther than that, and stayed near the lows much longer. This is, in part, because the market for entire companies is much less 'efficient' and therefore more susceptible to changes in sentiment and liquidity.

How Long Does It Take to Sell a Company? Depending on whom you ask, and whether they are trying to sell you something, you will get different answers on how long it takes to sell a company.

The time to exit depends a lot on the company – primarily on how long it will take to get the company into a saleable state, and then how much time the senior team has available to work with the M&A advisor.

A good rule of thumb is that it will take six to eighteen months from making the decision to completing the sale. Therefore, in order to execute the best exit, the decision to sell has to be made that long before achieving the peak in corporate value.

Timing your exit – Don't ride it over the top.
By Basil Peters

Most entrepreneurs wait too long to start thinking about their exit. They usually sell their companies for much less than they could have.

That's exactly what I did in my first company. It was the first time I lost several million dollars, and the first of many similarly expensive – and valuable – lessons about exits.

Most of the technology companies I've known well exited too late. Yes, most. *Riding it over the top* is by far the most common exit scenario. The primary cause is simply our fundamental human nature.

I recently met with two bright entrepreneurs who are building a company in an exciting niche market riding on a long term trend. These two young founders chose their space well and were already global leaders in their niche. They had prototypes in the market and a respectable global mind share.

Their niche was heating up quickly – unfortunately for them. In the previous six months, I'd read several articles in finance blogs or newsletters about yet another company that had just been financed in their specific vertical. Most of the financings I read about were for $5 million to $20 million. In contrast, this local company had been built on something around $1 million in equity.

This is a scenario I've seen about a hundred times before - too much money flushing into a space the VCs think will be hot. Too many companies being founded with exactly the same business plan.

These entrepreneurs were too young to attract the amount of capital they'd need to compete in this new environment. They had only two strategic options – an early exit, or hiring a 'name CEO' that might be able to raise a big enough round in time. I recommended an exit because I knew the money flowing in to their space would also increase valuations – possibly by 2x to 5x over normal ranges.

You can probably guess the young entrepreneurs wanted to wait a 'little longer.'

I don't want to be too hard on these young entrepreneurs. They were mostly victims of their own human nature.

They just couldn't think about selling because they were having too much fun. They were leaders in their market and big companies were enquiring about huge orders. They knew their revenues were getting ready to grow – and possibly explode.

Unfortunately, they couldn't appreciate that it was also the absolute best time to sell their company. In fact, they should have started the exit process six to twelve months earlier.

Human nature also affects the buyers. They will always pay the most when everything is going perfectly and the future looks even brighter. The buyers' human nature also means that a skilled M&A advisor can usually sell for a lot more based on the 'promise' rather than the 'reality.'

And human nature works against the entrepreneurs on the downside. This one ends up costing most entrepreneurs and their investors a lot of money, because most of the time CEOs and boards wait until it's pretty clear that the company's value has peaked before starting the exit process. By the time the buyers get to serious price negotiations, it's also clear to them that the company's best days are behind it. And another six to eighteen months have passed, usually allowing the trend to extend even further.

With exits, like many things in business and life, timing can be (almost) everything.

A successful exit is a great measure of a good journey.

I've been involved with well over a dozen successful exits over the years, some of them with monstrous gains, some more modest. Then in addition, there are the exits that returned some portion of capital, but nothing more. And finally, there are the sad exits that were complete write-offs for the investors, regaining some portion of note-holder or creditor money in the process. I can tell you with great enthusiasm that the high gain exits are by far the most enjoyable in every way. There's almost always a closing party where the board, prime investors, attorneys and investment banker all get together to celebrate the victory. It is an exhilarating ending to a great journey. The entrepreneur, whether remaining to the end as CEO or not, is celebrated for his or her prescient timing, great vision and excellent execution of the plan. One such celebration was even characterized as "We stuck the pig!" - the overly enthusiastic celebration of an outcome larger than expected.

But I cannot recall ever attending a closing dinner for a sale in which we returned only a portion of the investor group's money. In fact, I don't recall any formal post-sale meeting at all; even to digest the lessons learned from the entire experience, a missed opportunity for all.

And there is the sad truth of the large percentage of early stage investments that die an unceremonious death, often with the entrepreneur-founder left with a bitter feeling that "if only" there had been more cash invested, more co-operation from board members, more time to get to market, more of something, then the outcome would have been much better for all.

Of course the successful outcome is preferable for all. But more importantly, it marks a passing of a successful journey by a team first formed by a visionary entrepreneur, usually attracting smart money from good investors, who together effectively planned growth and finally a great exit.

Whenever those forces come together, celebrate them and the team that brought them all together.

Create stakeholder loyalty when times are good.

There are several times when stakeholder loyalty is tested to the limit. For employees, a late or missed payroll is the ultimate test of corporate loyalty, divorced even from an employee's ability to make do without a paycheck. For investors, a subsequent down round at a lower valuation than the last, or an exit opportunity at a loss are all opportunities for the affected stakeholder to show a side that can sometimes shock an entrepreneur or CEO. Managers almost always believe that stakeholders understand the pressures of the business and the circumstance of the present. The truth is that many employees merely make a simple pact: timely pay for time in service. If there is no closer connection to the corporation, when times are tough for any reason, it is these employees that make it tough for management to gain understanding and consent for actions that must be made such as missing payrolls, making layoffs, or abandoning pre-announced plans. And it is that disconnected employee, usually one or more of the better performers, that starts looking for a job when times look bad for a company.

Sometimes a secondary fund-raising effort leads to a lower valuation than the last. Although the investment documents from the previous round call for each investor group to vote as a class for or against new rounds of funding, in a contentious environment even a company in desperate need of new funding may find itself warring with its investors. I have seen investors allow a company to die, rather than suffer the massive dilution of an offer by a new investor.

And I have seen good offers from buyers of a company blocked by investors whose vote is needed to enable any such transaction, usually because these later investors would have a less-than-stellar exit with the sale, even if the founders would make out extremely well. That one hurts early investors and founders more than perhaps any other action by investors.

The message here is simple. By keeping stakeholders close with constant information as to the progress and even stressful setbacks, and by never withholding bad news, stakeholders will be in a much better position to understand necessary actions by senior management, and accede to decisions made in the best interest of the company, even at the expense of self. This kind of loyalty is never created during the bad times when everyone is thinking only of protecting self. Take advantage of the good times to build such loyalty.

Everyone wants to leave a legacy.

Be honest now. Have you ever thought of what legacy you'll leave behind? If you are an entrepreneur or CEO, surely you've thought of how you'll be remembered by your associates and stakeholders after you move on.

We've all heard the stories of tough SOB bosses that took advantage of employees, vendors, even stock holders. And such stories do get around. How many people who know those stories are willing to trust their next chapter to that person's next act? In my past, I made it a practice to hold exit interviews personally with nearly all separating employees, gaining insights from them they would not be willing to share while still employed with the company. And invariably, I'd end each with a handshake and the admonition: "I want us to part as friends. We never know how we're going to meet again, perhaps with the shoe on the other foot." I did not know for many years, until a most successful reunion planned by my former executives bringing back over a hundred past employees, how much that and other signs of respect and dignity for the employee-associate made our workplace rare and desirable.

I used to receive a list of birthdays for the next month from my assistant, culling the information from the corporate books spanning offices in many countries. Once a month, I would maintain the ritual of going to the local gift shop and buying enough birthday cards to fit each employee or associate. And once a month, while watching TV, I spend part of an evening writing personal messages to each birthday employee, recalling an event or complimenting a behavior or success. Such amazing accidental returns for such a small gesture. Even today, years later, I am met at industry events by former employees with a common refrain, "Our company was the best employer I have ever had, before or since."

That is a legacy you cannot buy, at a cost of acknowledging individuals with respect and personal recognition. And what do I remember about that ten-plus year experience, among the thrills of rapid growth, great workplace, and great lucrative exit? Most of all, it is those personal moments of contact with former employees, each recalling with appreciation their time at our company.

Do you engage an investment banker?

Many CEOs have asked me if I felt an investment banker adds value if the buyer has already been identified.

Investment bankers sometimes slow the process by requiring a "deal book" to be prepared containing considerable information about a company to help a buyer. Deal books are expensive to create.

Other investment bankers insist that the company create competition for a deal, even if the buyer has already submitted a letter of interest to the seller. Competition opens the deal to more public access, slows the deal and could give competitors wind of an otherwise confidential process. And yet, it is almost universally acknowledged that without competition for a deal, the price will be lower, sometimes much lower.

Then there is the question of fees. For small deals, an investment banker will ask as much as ten percent, although the average is slightly above half that. For larger deals, expect the fee to start at five percent and scale downward with size. And expect the investment banker to ask for an advance against expenses of at least $20,000 or much more with larger deals, with any unexpended funds not to be refunded. If a buyer is already in hand, many will work for far less in percentage fees, and even in advances, because much of their work is done at that point.

And there is the question of whether an investment banker has a personal agenda to get a deal done in minimum time, even if the proceeds to the seller are less than could have been expected. Is there any conflict of interest? Is this not a parallel to the question of a real estate agent who cares little about that last five or ten percent of the purchase price, if it would kill a deal or slow its close, since the agent's commission amount is only a fraction of that difference?

And finally, could not the corporate attorney do just as good a job of negotiating a great deal for the seller, and do it for hourly rates instead of a percent of the transaction?

My experience is that good investment bankers do add significant value to a deal in most cases, easily earning multiples of their fee by increasing competition, upping the price, and finding areas for extra value that the seller did not think of. Good investment bankers work with your attorney to structure the deal, help the seller to see more of the value hidden in the candidate seller, and increase the sense of urgency to close the deal among all parties.

Perhaps most of all, a good investment banker will insulate the seller CEO against the anger and ire of the buyer during the process that always accompanies stressful negotiations or issues revolving around the seller CEO's continuing employment contract. Imagine you're fighting with the buyer CEO about your expected salary and benefits during a transition period to follow, expecting to work harmoniously with that CEO after all the tension and conflicts during the negotiation of the deal. And imagine having that buffer in the form of the investment banker arguing on your behalf while you sit silently, giving up little or no good will during the maelstrom around you. Presented with these mental pictures and the recommendations from so many of us that have done deals with and without investment bankers, you may lean toward interviewing a group of your industry's best for the size of your deal, and being convinced that creating such a team is a good investment.

Start a deal room and keep it current.

Maybe you have not heard the term, "deal book." That's a comprehensive piece on a company for use by a buyer in determining fit. A "deal room" is an electronic or physical space dedicated to storing the massive amounts of data to be used in due diligence by a buyer, lender or by an investor.

Deal rooms contain access to or copies of all significant contracts with suppliers, customers, consultants, and others. All corporate governance documents, from incorporation articles to minutes of all meetings of the board are maintained in the deal room. Up-to-date insurance policies, leases, financial documents and schedules such as fixed assets are copied here. Copies of intellectual property filings such as patents, copyrights and trademarks, all owned URL addresses, and even copies of source code, may be resident in the deal room, dependent upon the type of buyer. Current documents relating to any lawsuits by or against the company are maintained there as well.

In this day of electronic record-keeping, access to the deal room is available remotely by a buyer with appropriate access, saving the long and expensive personal visits by lawyers, accountants and others to the seller's facility. Well-maintained deal rooms enhance a company's image with a buyer, quicken the pace of the deal, help maintain secrecy from employees while due diligence is in process, and lower the stress levels of all parties during the process.

But maintaining such an electronic or physical facility is time-consuming and costly. The question is whether to start this exhausting process early in the life of a corporation, or rush to complete it when a deal is identified or the run to a sale is imminent.

Because deal rooms have multiple applications, the best advice is to begin the process right after incorporation and make keeping it current a continuing job of your financial senior management. Whether it means copying physical printouts and creating volumes in three-ring binders or scanning documents and creating electronic folders, incremental additions are much easier to make than an all-out run at the finish.

Bankers, investors, strategic partners, and ultimately your buyer or even attorneys providing opinions for an IPO, will all be most impressed by your thoughtful early management decision to make their lives easier and their job more productive.

Leave something on the table in a sale.

Isn't the goal of any negotiation to get the maximum possible out of the other side? I have learned from long experience that the last bit of concession is the most expensive in a negotiation. Invariably, it's after the negotiation, whether during the final documentation of the deal or after the closing when the buyer finds those unexpected surprises, and that the seller who drives the hardest bargain is the one attacked with the most energy by the affronted buyer.

Certainly, sales contracts usually call for a basket or amount of findings below which the buyer will absorb the costs. The problem comes when the buyer finds surprises that could have much greater effect, but whose cost will not be known for years. Customer contracts that come up for renewal but are not renewed as expected, a customer bankruptcy after the closing, a group of employees that leave together to start a new business. There are so many unforeseen opportunities to make a buyer unhappy after the closing, that it is good strategy to leave enough on the table, labeled carefully as such, so that there is no doubt as to the "gift" from the seller. As a percentage of the total package, often such a gesture is small, but the benefit can be great if the unexpected happens.

Money is not the only measure of success.

You've surely heard of Maslow's Hierarchy of Needs, in which Abraham Maslow laid out a human's needs from the physiological first, to safety, then love and belonging, on to esteem and finally self-actualization. Assuming that you have now passed through the hallowed hall of a successful sale and the money is in the bank, enough to at least temporarily satisfy your needs, if not much more, in Maslow's Hierarchy. You have arrived at the point where you can think about love, belonging, esteem and self-actualization.

I have great respect for the young entrepreneur CEO of the game company I described in insight 93, because he disciplined himself enough to take extensive time for family after the closing of the sale, increasing his participation in all things family.

During our business formation years, we pay much more attention to the enterprise than we know we should, at the expense of family and community. I propose that there are few times in life when the opportunity opens to look only outward, to participate in charity events, extended family vacations, community boards and even coaching other entrepreneurs.

If you ever have the opportunity to experience the simple power of having few personal worries, you will have known the freedom of choice that allows you to reinvent yourself, dividing your attention between people and organizations outside of your previous circles. How empowering. And how many organizations are in need of management skills and relationships such as those you could bring, along perhaps with a new focus upon philanthropy.

Maslov demonstrated it as well as can be done. Beyond some point, whatever that is for you, money is not the only measure of success.

The most satisfying life journey is never about the money.

As I look back over more than fifty years as an entrepreneur, I can think of the financial focus of my three entrepreneurial businesses as a prime driver in my life during the early stage of each. And yet, as I recall the greatest thrills, the memorable events, the best of memories, almost none are about the money. The stories of people rising to the occasion, victories in the form of great sale successes, great continuing relationships, occasional awards from valued industry or academic institutions, being able to give back to those who appreciate the gift of time or money – all seem to rise well above the feeling recalled about the check or wire transfer that represented a completed sale of a company.

I found one of my joys in angel investing, putting money to work by investing time and money into promising young entrepreneurs much like I once was, coaching them, putting them together with others who have needed skills, helping to build someone else's dream. If you are in such a good place in your life, find a local angel investing group by Googling "angel investing". You will find such a group near enough to drive to their periodic meetings. You'll quickly be drawn into the governance of the organization and introduced into the process of discovery, coaching, leading deals, herding investors, serving on boards and helping entrepreneurs toward liquidity events.

I found another joy in community organizations, joining a total of four non-profit boards, learning at first much more than I could teach, but rising over the years to leadership positions with large psychic rewards along each step of the way.

And then there is family. Be honest with yourself. Have you ever spent enough time with your family? Can you ever? Isn't it time to try?

For those of you still struggling to find that security, to find that balance, I wish you all the skills and all the success possible. For those with the blessing of time and room to breathe, I wish you the wisdom and energy to make use of this most valuable gift. Your most satisfying journey will never be about the money.

Don't be greedy even if you have the power.

Sometimes the end game or sale of the company is not a happy event. Especially when outside investors, venture capitalists, or angels, have put in substantial money and the sales price is less than the value of their investment. Most all experienced VC and angel investors have found themselves in such a situation, since it is the unfortunate truth that half of their investments fail, on average, within the first several years of the investment.

There are a number of questions a distressed sale brings to mind. Does the board declare dividends upon the preferred stock invested in order to increase the amount paid out to the preferred - at the expense of the common – shareholders, which usually includes the founder(s)? Is there a liquidation preference in place where the preferred investors can take a multiple of their investment, (twice or three times the amount) from a sale before the common shares receive anything? Is there a participation clause in the investment agreement where, even after the preferred shareholders take their share, their stock also converts into common stock and participates (again) alongside the common shareholders?

I have been on a number of boards where just these decisions are faced, often with the corporate attorney in the room as protection, with the specter of conflict of interest looming over the discussion, as board members who are preferred investors decide how to divide the proceeds of a marginal sale of the company or its assets.

A recent decision by the Delaware Court in favor of the common shareholders in marginal sales sheds light upon this dilemma for boards – at least for boards of Delaware corporations, no matter where they reside.

The Trados Decision (Delaware Court of Chancery) protects the common and early stage investors even if the late stage investors can claim all from a sale with their liquidation preferences. Directors can be held liable under certain circumstances for favoring the interests of preferred shareholders over common stockholders. This raises the bar for venture capitalists in a marginal sale of a business. It brings forward the question of conflicts of interest between VC investor board members and the shareholders they are legally bound to protect.

And yet, VCs sometimes bravely put in more money near the end of the life of a company to bridge the company to a sale of assets in an attempt to recover some or all of the original investment. This late money is at much higher risk to the VCs than even the early stage investments that were optimistically made by angels or friends and family. Most of the time, this late money is advanced in the form of a loan, and all loans are paid out of funds before any investors receive their first dollar of return. When this is the situation and the proceeds of a sale are too small to cover even the loan, there is no conflict between shareholders and note holders or VCs.

As the amounts recovered from the marginal sale increase, the conflict of interest problem becomes more acute.

Guided by the Trados Decision, preferred investors should think twice before exercising the full amount of their documented preferences in a marginal sale, volunteering to leave some of the proceeds for common shareholders, perhaps in a negotiated agreement once the amounts are known and absolute. This is rare today, but with the court decision in place, may become more of an issue in the future.

Of course, once the amounts from a sale or IPO exceed all the preferences by a substantial amount, everyone is happier since the preferred shareholders must either take their multiple of investment or convert to common, losing their preferred preferences, and participate ratably (or equally) with all the common shareholders. These are events to celebrate, since it certainly was the intent of all parties at the point of original investment to witness the day when just such a split of the proceeds would occur.

Failure is the greatest of teachers.

Not all companies are successful. The end game can be a failure of the business. In fact, many angel investors or venture capitalists look for and respect the lessons learned by entrepreneurs that have survived a failed business. The key question is how did the entrepreneur fail? And then: What lessons were learned from the failure?

One VC calls this entrepreneur one who "has seen the movie before" and spends time questioning the entrepreneur on lessons learned, often praising the person for having figured out the issues leading to the failure. Yes, it works both ways. A successful entrepreneur who has seen the movie before is even more valued. But in these days of fast failures, and with the knowledge that 50% of all startups do fail within a few years of formation, there is a lot of learning to be had out there.

Questions to be asked include: "What were the major factors contributing to the failure?" "How quickly did you and your team change the plan when faced with the first signs?" "Did you seek outside guidance?"

Most failed entrepreneurs blame undercapitalization for the cause of the failed business. Investors do not like to hear this excuse, even if absolutely true. Any business can use more money. It is up to management to scale the development, marketing and production based upon resources available.

But sometimes, that includes the promise of investment or loans upon reaching milestones, and occasionally the investor does not fulfill those promises. There are lessons to be learned about reliance upon outside investors, early use of limited resources, and communication with investors, all to be gleaned from such experiences.

So consider a failure as an opportunity. Some will flee to safety and seek a stable job in the wake of a failure. Others, often serial entrepreneurs, will carefully think out the experience and vow not to repeat it, creating an intellectual advantage over others making their run in the establishment of a new venture.

A million things can kill the deal.

So you've found the buyer, received a letter of interest, signed it, and tied your company up for a period to complete the deal. Everyone on the board is anxious to close this. You've committed time to do whatever is needed. You've informed your top management of the pending deal and they know they will be impacted and are a bit skittish. You wonder if you should make a public announcement to your troops, worrying over loss of focus, people thinking of jumping ship, competitors finding morsels of weakness to exploit.

Welcome to the club. If you're seeing this movie for the first time from the top, you need to ask many questions and be led by your outside team, whether legal, financial, accounting, or networking – or all. The months between the LOI and the closing are as stressful as any you will experience as a CEO, and there are few ways to reduce the stress.

First, should you inform your employees of the deal? You know that the buyer will be crawling the offices with legal and accounting personnel, reviewing contracts, financials, governance documentation, intellectual property, leases, and much more. How do you explain this if not by making a general announcement?

Let's back up to the headline. "A million things can kill the deal" is a statement from an experienced professional, and worth listening to. During the due diligence period, before the signing of the definitive documents and establishing the closing date, it is not wise to make a general announcement, and certainly not wise to make a press release. Public companies are forced to release this information in most cases after the LOI is signed, and this may impact you if being purchased by a public entity.

What could happen to kill the deal that looks so good to all now? For starters, as the due diligence and documentation period drags on, you'll have to keep your company's eyes off the ball to continue the increasing revenues and profit momentum. A bad quarter in the middle of the process will certainly lead to the buyer either withdrawing the offer or more likely reducing the price, sometimes to a point that is unacceptable to you.

Few companies are squeaky clean. And in this age of Dodge-Cox and Sarbanes-Oxley regulation, public companies are thrown by any hint of activities that might have seemed all right in the past world of private enterprise, but don't fit with the regulations on public corporations today. Paying commissions to undisclosed third parties in order to obtain deals, hiding or entering misleading financial data, associating with anyone with a past SEC suspension, and many more "gotcha" events, qualify as strong deterrents to a good closing.

Events that you cannot control such as changes in the buyer's circumstance, a drop in the market price of the buyer's stock, a bad quarter at the buyer's shop, all can contribute to abandonment of a good deal.

Both sides have to work to get a deal closed. Professional advice before and during the process is necessary. No one is able to do this alone, especially a CEO who is involved and too close to see many of these issues.

Share your liquidity success with those who got you there.

Some companies have good, formal stock option plans with properly priced options set to reward all in the event of a corporate sale. Usually, the higher the ranks, the more the options held and therefore the greater reward at exit. If there has never been outside investors to organize such an option program, many CEOs never get around to creating a system for rewarding employees in a sale.

I found myself in such a situation upon a sale of my computer software company. There was no question that each of the five vice presidents had been greatly responsible for our success and getting us to the successful exit. Yet there was no formal reward in place other than the employee stock ownership program (ESOP) which was set to pay all employees for their accumulated shares at the exit. So I wrote into the final distribution instructions a surprise five figure bonus for each of the five executives. Each was surprised, pleased and effusive. Upon reflection, I should have given each even more.

Turning out the lights is a type of exit.

In my life as an early stage investor, I've been closely involved with so many businesses, there were bound to be numerous stories of failures, hopefully from which to learn lessons for all of us as we go forward.

Several times in my investing life, as the final board member making the arrangements to dispose of remaining assets, I have literally been the one to turn out the lights, carry out the books and records to my car, and become the only remaining contact between the failed business and the investors, bankruptcy court, or creditors.

In aviation circles, we read in our pilot magazines about "Never again!" or "I learned about flying from that." Pilot-authors tell their stories in the first person, and all of us readers slow down to think while reading of these events, wondering "what if" or whether this could happen to me. And if it did, would I have reacted differently? Most importantly, we think: 'Now that I know this, would I behave differently if it did happen to me?'

So that is why we devote the next several insights to just this subject. Professional investors rarely attach a red letter upon a failed entrepreneur. In fact, if that person can tell his or her story and relate the lessons learned clearly, there is a positive response many of us will make to the next pitch from that person.

We who invest look for patterns from previous experience. Some of those patterns help us to spot and avoid problems we have seen play out in the past, often to disastrous conclusion. We learn to worry over obsolete inventory, too rapid hiring, failure to spot industry trends that make an offering less attractive, and so much more. Most of us can tell specific stories of losses that led to these expensive and gut-wrenching lessons.

In past insights, we have explored many aspects of preparation for and execution of a great exit. Let's spend a few cycles learning from the words of an eloquent, driven entrepreneur as he tells first hand his story of his failed business, followed by an analysis by yet another entrepreneur who knew the first, adding valuable insight about the problems, the failure to act upon trends, and more.

My story and what I learned from losing it all.
By Eric Greenspan

Eric Greenspan is a consummate entrepreneur and blogger. His company, Make It Work, was a significant presence in California major metropolitan areas for over a decade, and attracted numerous rounds of angel investment over the years.

Eleven years and eight months of commitment, my life savings, every available dollar on every credit card, line and loan, and a promise to my children of a future, all gone. The real story behind my company's demise isn't exciting. It's simply about a team of dedicated individuals that failed.

We failed because the industry we were in changed over the years. We failed because the economy drastically fell into recession, particularly in the consumer sector. We failed because Apple invented the iPad and the Genius Bar. We failed because Microsoft finally got Windows right. We failed because we tried. We gave it everything we had and it in turn, it took everything we had.

Ours was an amazing company. With over 38,000 cult-like testimonials, one cannot dispute the company delivered a valuable service in a way like no other company has come close. Sadly, it will probably not be remembered this way.

As co-founder and CEO, I take responsibility. In doing so, I will assume all of the personally guaranteed loans and lines granted to the company. I personally guaranteed these loans, because I believed we could not fail. I was wrong.

The company had been forced to lower its prices, to meet competition and find acceptance. Additionally, over the years margins got smaller and eventually, stopped making sense. We worked tirelessly to find solutions to maintaining growth and profitability, critical components of any business.

The company was always seeking capital. As an entrepreneur, my greatest lesson learned here was how difficult it is to find capital for a services business. Venture capital firms have a distaste for the smaller multiples earned by services businesses, along with the challenge to scale such a business. As a result, the company was always under-capitalized.

For three years, the company paid its own bills. We were cash flow positive and we believed we could maintain this trend indefinitely. But then, new customers slowed, appointment bookings slowed and average appointment time dropped. The company raised some capital to supplement, shifted its business model, reduced its overhead, and sought new lines of business. During this period, the greatest opportunity in the company's history came into play. We were exuberant about a new relationship with a retail giant, which could offer our computer repair and installation services through their stores. We expected significant growth and anticipated the company to emerge as solvent, profitable and wildly successful. This didn't happen, but it also wasn't the end.

In May of our last year in operation, sales dropped drastically. After a solid April, we figured this was just the cycles of business. We sought capital just in case. Then June came and the downward trend continued. We continued to seek capital, launched aggressive discounted promotions and forged ahead.

Then, we got a verbal yes on a decent capital investment. We worked towards closing it. Sales remained sluggish during this period, but we were not giving up. We'd been here before, but never with an opportunity like the retail distribution contract with a big box chain, using their significant website, sitting in our lap. We were certain the funding would come through. Days went by; we stayed focused. Meanwhile, we were working on the big box retail store launch. We were so close to getting the funding. We needed it badly.

The leasing company wanted a payment. In a few days, our payroll that we had never missed in our eleven years was at risk. On that same Friday, our insurance lapsed, and we were forced to ground the fleet of 31 cars. Then came the weekend; our lease payment and payroll were both due Monday. On Sunday, around noon, the investor backed out. We immediately informed our board and shareholders that we were forced to halt operations. Monday came and the leasing company arrived to take our fleet. We missed payroll. It was over.

I immediately called every press outlet to be proactive in telling our story, changed our website to inform our customers; and our few remaining staff fielded calls and emails from our customers. There wasn't much more we could do.

Did we make mistakes along the way? You bet we did; plenty of them. But we learned and we grew and we fought against the current. At the end of the day, I'm not sure it would've mattered. The trend of self-healing, do-it-yourself installations and solid state devices will only make matters worse for our competitors. Apple changed the world.

Profit from the lessons learned from total loss.
By Eric Rhoads

Eric Rhoads is an entrepreneur founder of several businesses and is chairman of Streamline Publishing, a media company with conferences, print and electronic publications, video, and books.

We all know how hard EG and his team worked. They thought of every angle and attacked each with vigor. At the end of the day the team faced something every business faces, and often we're too close or too stubborn to see: *change*. Yes of course the economy had an impact as it has with all of us. Yet sometimes a bad economy reveals what a good economy masks. Great sales can hide problems. Poor sales make us pay close attention to our pennies, which we should be doing all along.

The greatest challenge a small business owner can face is that change happens fast. We often cling to our ideas that work, and refuse to adjust because we think the trend we're seeing is a result of something else (the economy for instance). When we see some success, we tend to increase our payrolls before we really should, and the biggest mistake is thinking more money will solve our problems. Sometimes having lots of capital simply speeds us up, so we hit the wall more quickly.

Having been in this position and barely squeaking by on three different occasions, I can tell you that EG is feeling a tremendous amount of pain at the moment and he's probably frightened about how to raise his family and possibly fearful about whether or not to do this again.

America is full of great business guys like him who have been slammed down. The smart ones realize that this is the greatest experience of their careers, and that this experience will lead them to success if they are smart enough to examine what went wrong.

The first and most important thing is to accept the blame and not blame it on circumstances. Sure, circumstances played a role, but it's the nimble CEO who watches her or his money, trends, sales, and business acceleration, and is willing to slam on the breaks at high speed and make a sudden left turn, and hope it's the right decision. Though employees usually will tell you all the reasons you're wrong, most entrepreneurs and managers making quick decisions will tell you that anything good they did was met with employee resistance.

EG is a brilliant guy who will pick himself up, dust off the pain, and understand there is no shame in having to close a company. Though it's hard to recover, hard to face investors, hard to face family, it's important to clear his head of the angst caused by this tragedy and start working on the next idea.

The average multi-millionaire will tell you that he or she has failed two or three times before becoming successful. Failure is nothing more than a tool for growth. There is no shame in failure, and just like steel, strengthened by fire, EG and others like him will be better, stronger entrepreneurs or managers because of this experience.

When this first success happened to me I started living large. I was driving a car I thought I could afford. I was working on plans for a mega-house. I was spending more than I should and hiring more people than I should because I thought it would last, and thought I was a genius - until the day my bookkeeper told me "Eric, you'll be bankrupt in about six weeks." Thank Goodness I had six weeks, and rather than denial I immediately terminated fifty people and reduced to a staff of four.

Advisors told me I would be better off to just close the business because there was no way I could survive. It was painful, the start of a very long dry period. We almost did not make it with only four to do the work of many more. But we got through it, and when we came out of it we were stronger, and realized that we never needed that many people. We were forced to reinvent and develop ways to become more efficient and then became highly profitable.

I like and respect EG, and I wish he did not have to go through this. But perhaps it's the best thing that can happen to a young business owner early in their career. It will make him stronger, and if he avoids the traps of allowing expenses to creep up in the future, he will be just fine.

Sell when growth is high, even if cash flow is low.
By John Huston

There are only two types of companies -those which have achieved positive cash flow and those which have not. *(Earnings Before Interest, Taxes, Depreciation and Amortization, or EBITDA is the most commonly used definition of cash flow.)*

While it is easy to divide all companies into just these two groups, this simplification ignores whether management has made a conscious, strategic choice about their growth. Perhaps you have decided to continue growing top line revenues at the expense of cash flow (EBITDA.) For high growth ventures being groomed for a lucrative liquidity event, this is usually a wise choice, presuming additional growth capital can be successfully raised on agreeable terms.

The issue is whether your company could pare back expenses and live within the cash it is currently generating - if you had to do so. This should be a major milestone goal of all start-ups. Until it is reached, survival still hinges on the kindness of outside funding sources.

But this too is an overly simplistic view. Usually leading up to the time positive cash flow is initially reached, the management team is not taking a market wage, payables are stretched, and any slowing of receivables collections would likely cause layoffs. The team knows their current expenses are being so closely managed, that at some point they would be unable to continue in this mode. They have achieved a level of cash generation which enables "survival" - but it is not sustainable.

Now that you are more mature as a business, management can decide how to balance building revenues versus building cash flow. There is a point at which building cash flow above revenues yields diminishing investor returns considering the amount of capital and time it consumes. Furthermore, having substantial positive cash flow may sub-optimize investor returns at the exit. This is because potential acquirers often act like mere financial buyers when they see a significant positive cash flow stream. This prompts them to merely apply a multiple (often 5 – 8X) to the EBITDA or cash flow of the business, always a smaller number than when pricing an acquisition for strategic reasons. So, rarely will this strategy or outcome enable investors to reap their target in a sale.

Ventures which have negative EBITDA, *but could turn it positive if they chose to do so*, are exhibiting the growth which attracts more bidders. Those which generate high returns at the exit are often not sporting positive cash flow when sold, *but they could dial back to be positive if required.* They are demonstrating by their actions that bidders cannot bid low, because by bidding low buyers would be assuming that a sale is necessary due to the company's negative cash flow.

The bottom line: Looking at best example companies in a sale, their acquisition strategy was to avoid growing their cash flow before the exit. Counterintuitive perhaps, but demonstrated to be effective.

Solve partnership issues before the company sale.
By William de Temple

William De Temple is a seasoned executive with experience in turn-around and start-up ventures. As CEO of Maximize Management, Inc., he oversees work with turn-around and growth company clients nationwide. William is also founder of The Enterprise Training Academy.

This is a story about a company I became involved with, preparing for a sale as a way to resolve conflicts between two brothers who couldn't agree on how to manage their business.

The company was just three years old, already managing $7 million in revenues, and generating 23% in net income. And the company was in chaos. The company was structured as an LLC with each brother owning half interest. Three years before, they had self-incorporated to save a few dollars.

The older brother was the more experienced, having built a previous business to nearly $6 million before the 2008 recession wiped out that business. He was focused upon growth, reinvestment of profit, and special handling of employees as a prime asset. The younger brother had been a car dealer, treating his sales people like disposable assets, and unwilling to spend upon infrastructure or employee benefits.

The two brothers could not agree on much of anything. The rift between them grew so wide that the older brother refused to come into the office when the younger brother was present. It appeared that only a sale of the company could solve the growing problem of complete disagreement about management style and spending decisions. So I was brought in to prepare the company for sale.

As I began doing my due diligence to prepare a sales package, I found most everything I needed was missing. There was no membership agreement. The employee records were shoddy at best. They were keeping their books on a weekly basis rather than a monthly basis, making it difficult to do year to year comparisons. And they pulled out the bulk of the profits on a weekly basis rather than drawing a salary or declaring a distribution before year end. Nearly all the equipment had been brought over from the older brother's previous company and had never been recorded on the books of the new company.

It took much additional time and money to begin to bring the company into a place where it could be offered for sale. Unfortunately, this is not a unique story. It takes little extra effort to maintain generally acceptable accounting records, to incorporate without errors, and to keep a clean record of assets. These two paid the price for not doing so with an extended sales cycle and many months of continued tension between them, all of which was avoidable with a bit of pre-planning at the start of the relationship.

Don't be greedy even if you can.

Sometimes the end game or sale of the company is not a happy event for the early investors, including the entrepreneur or the founders. Especially when outside investors, venture capitalists or angels have put in substantial money, and the sales price is not enough to give them a reasonable return for the time and money invested, these investors can be – in a word – greedy.

Most sophisticated investors will take either a promissory note or preferred stock, both of which come before founder or management stock in a sale or liquidation. Promissory notes come before any equity, and most late equity investments come before early equity investments, even of the same class of security. This makes for some head-rubbing when attempting to calculate the return on investment with a proposed sale. Further, preferred stock holders can be recipient of accrued dividends in a sale or liquidation. A rather common but small dividend rate of six percent becomes a massive amount after seven years, almost half again the value of the original investment. And some preferred investors have participation rights, where they take all of the above amounts, and then also convert their shares into common stock and participate again alongside the founders and option holders.

It is in this combination of possible methods of amassing a return that greed can become a significant factor, so much so that the courts are sometimes stepping in to void some of the most onerous terms of investment agreements when challenged by those locked out of payment in a sale.

Take a situation where the VC investors finally see the chance of a return after ten years, with participating preferred and fifty percent of the ownership after several rounds. A marginal sale at twice their original invested amount could yield a starting value of eighty percent of the sales price to the VCs (fifty percent invested plus accumulated dividends for ten years at six percent which equals thirty percent of the sale price) and then fifty percent of the remaining twenty percent after participation. The result is that the preferred shareholders would receive ninety percent of a sales price that was double their investment, compared to ten percent shared by the founders and all others, including option holder-employees.

No-one complains if the sales price is ten times the investment, since there is plenty to go around. It is in these marginal sales that the formula distorts returns so badly in favor of the investors.

Fortunately, and perhaps because the courts have not looked favorably upon these outcomes, many VCs will voluntarily forgive either accumulated dividends or participation in a marginal sale, especially if the sale is cultivated, planned and carried out by the efforts of the common shareholders including the founders.

Although many VCs are openly against allocating a "cutout" for management in marginal sales, practically speaking, management must be taken care of in marginal sales, or the sale might not happen at all. In a cutout, some percentage, usually fifteen or twenty percent of the total sale, is allocated to management in order to continue operations through the closing period and help in closing the sale. That further reduces the amount available to founders if not still in the ranks of management.

So this advice is directed to the investors. *Don't be greedy even if you can.* You will not be moving your IRR needle enough by grabbing a few extra dollars in a marginal sale, but you will incur the wrath of a number of stakeholders who would be more than willing to spread the word far and wide about your greedy ways. And that reputation will last for a long time in the entrepreneurial community.

Conversely, I have praised and seen others praise VCs who volunteer to eliminate participation clauses even before knowing the ultimate sales price in a deal. It is those who receive the loudest accolades since they have given up a right for the good of the rest of the investor and management community.

The muted thrill of the deal closing.

Now you have worked for months to get this deal to the closing, anticipating the wire transfers to the shareholders that will come any minute. This could change your life style and give you that much needed pause in your life you have been looking forward to.

All the documents were signed in a rolling series of emailed scanned signature pages during the past week or more, with each party signing their own set, never having to be in the same room to sign the single signature page for each agreement. And in the end, the deal that means so much to you closes with a whisper. You check your bank account every half hour to see if the wire has been posted.

Finally it arrives and you see the balance in your account jump to a number you've never seen there before. You pause for a minute to savor the victory. And you go back to what you were doing right before that moment. Or not. But the closing was such a non-event that you wonder why people even call it a "closing."

Congratulations. You have joined an exclusive club, and have earned your membership.

It used to be thrilling to participate in a real "live" closing. The date and time of the closing would be published for all interested parties. The lawyers for both buyer and seller would meet the day before to go over a "trial closing" to be sure all documents were ready to sign. And on the appointed morning, often at 10 AM, all attorneys, the investment bankers, you and your buyer's CEO would all gather in a large conference room with documents already spread around the conference table. After pleasantries, you and your opposite CEO would pick up your (fountain) pens and start moving around the table, signing agreements in the appointed spots until your fingers were weak from the effort. The lawyers would follow and check, then finally all nod that the work was done. A handshake, applause, a promise to meet the next day, and a celebration closing meal either immediately following or at a future time sealed the deal for all.

Those were the days. The smell of the newly-copied papers, the smudges from the fountain pen ink, the tension followed by smiles all around, all contributed to the feeling that something grand was happening.

My favorite closing followed this pattern with a twist. There must have been 25 of us that arrived for a 4:00 PM closing after the day-before trial closing by the attorneys. We all expected to be finished and out of there for a late dinner. At five the next morning, after an all-night session with revisions, midnight calls to the buyer's parent CEO in New York and more, we finally signed the papers, all completely worn out from the many anxious moments and long, long night. All the parties vowed to go home and get some sleep. I went home, took a shower, and went to work as if a typical day, working now as CEO of a subsidiary of a parent company. And yes, I checked the bank account every half hour for the wire transfer. Some things do not change.

For those of you who ever experience the muted thrill of today's electronic closing, you can give a nod to those days when the smoke-filled rooms were real and the tension palatable, when a closing was a face to face event.

Take the time to celebrate your exit.

We come to the end of this book of insights with a thought about how you might view your successful exit from the company you have spent so much effort to build.

You've worked hard for years to reach the payoff, and the money sure looks good as you contemplate the wire transfer to come, and then watch your bank account fill to a level you only dreamed of during those rough cash flow years. You might even allow yourself to admit that you almost lost it all several times during this long run, and that only you knew how close you came to the abyss. But you did make it, and that's what counts.

Whether the exit was as large as you hoped, or whether your goals of taking care of all the people who helped you get to this point were realized, the exit itself generates a complex set of emotions in all of us.

First there comes a sense of relief, knowing that you no longer need to worry over daily cash or threats to your net worth. Then you experience a feeling of guilt when you realize that not all of your early associates share the same outcome, either financially or perhaps with their continued employment with the buyer.

Then you focus on the money in your bank account, smiling at the accomplishment of accumulating assets that are tangible and can be valued, perhaps for the first time.

But what most entrepreneurs fail dramatically at is to celebrate the moment. To celebrate with those who took the journey with you, with those closest to you who sacrificed as you spent those long hours away. To celebrate with your suppliers who helped you, especially during the rough times. To celebrate with your customers, who worry over continuity and look to you for assurances that the transition will not negatively affect them. And to celebrate for yourself, for making it all the way to the finish line.

Not many founders or entrepreneurs do experience the success of a favorable sale of the business they dreamed would make them rich. Many fail multiple times. Some fail in the first year of the attempt. Others are diluted by subsequent investors to the point where there was nothing for them to celebrate at all in a sale.

So as you prepare to turn over the reins to another; to separate from a business that has become a part of your being, it is time to think of nothing but the good done, the examples set, the positive company culture you leave behind.

As you begin to focus upon the future, remember the emotions, the lessons, the lasting friendships from the past. I often advise managers, CEOs and entrepreneurs always to part on a positive note and never burn the bridges of any past relationship. You'll never guess whom you'll meet in your next act, and how they will be able to contribute positively to your next success.

So celebrate your exit by reaching out to as many of those who've helped along the way as you can. Close this chapter of your life on the highest note possible. Take a long breath. The do as all good entrepreneurs do. Start dreaming of the next big idea. Take with you the best wishes from those in your past, and build upon the education you received with this effort.

Write a book; I did. Write a long hand letter to someone who helped you make it to the finish line. That extra effort will shock and please them. Call an early key employee and take that person to dinner as a thank you for those hard times.

Hit the beach. Pay attention to your family. Think about investments and tax efficiency. Go into a mental dark room and dream about your next act. Take a long breath, or weeks of long breaths. Exhale slowly. This is what a moment of reduced pressure and responsibility feels like. Savor that moment.

Then if it strikes you as right, start the process all over again. May you have only the greatest success in your next act, whatever that is and wherever it takes you.

Entrepreneurs do not easily retire.

So you've successfully sold your business and have received enough money from the sale to become financially independent, no longer having to work for a living. That is a comfortable place to be, and it is one experienced by more and more people, especially in technology-based businesses.

Most successful sales of businesses, again especially in the technology arena, enrich younger entrepreneurs and stock-option holders who are under fifty years of age. Having interviewed many of these newly-rich alumni, I have found that most want to take time off for an indefinite time to think out their next move, which is not a bad idea. Some immediately start to plan their next venture. And some tell me that they will just retire, finding travel, coaching, teaching and a life of leisure their most attractive alternative.

I followed many of these stated retirees, and very few if any retiring entrepreneurs stay that way for long. Their lifestyles may change, sometimes dramatically, but for a driven entrepreneur, a full stop is difficult over time.

Just saying…

About the author...

Dave Berkus has a proven track record in operations, venture investing and corporate board service, both public and private. As an entrepreneur, he has formed, managed and sold successful businesses in the entertainment and software arenas. As a private equity investor, he has obtained healthy returns from liquidity events in over a dozen investments in early-stage ventures. As a corporate mentor and director, he was named *"Director of the Year"* for his directorship efforts with over 40 companies in the past decade.

Dave was the founder of **Computerized Lodging Systems Inc.,** *(CLS),* which he guided as founder and CEO for over a decade that included two consecutive years on the *Inc.500* list of America's fastest growing companies, expansion to six foreign subsidiaries and twenty-nine foreign distributors, while capturing 16% of the world market for his enterprise products. Known as a hospitality industry visionary with many "firsts" to his credit and for his accomplishments in advancing technology in the hospitality industry, in 1998 he was inducted into the **Hospitality (HFTP) "International Hall of Fame,"** one of only thirty so honored worldwide over the years.

He has made over 100 investments in early stage ventures, for which he has an IRR of 97%, which includes capital contributions to his two funds (**Berkus Technology Ventures, LLC** and **Kodiak Ventures, L.P.**, for which he is the managing partner). He is also Chairman Emeritus of the Tech Coast Angels, one of the largest angel networks in the United States.

In recognition for adding significant shareholder value for emerging technology companies over the past decade, he was named **"Director of the Year-Early Stage Businesses"** by the *Forum for Corporate Directors* of Orange County, California and **"Technology Leader of the Year"** by the Los Angeles County Board of Supervisors. Dave currently sits on ten corporate boards and four non-profit boards.

About the author...

Dave is also a senior partner in the twenty year old consulting firm of *Hospitality Automation Consultants, LTD (HACL)*, and lends his considerable visionary and strategic talents to worldwide hospitality chains and groups. He is the partner responsible for business process reorganization, strategic planning, software development and wide-area network infrastructure, and enterprise management systems.

A graduate of Occidental College, Dave currently serves as a Trustee of the College. Aside from this book, he is author of fourteen other books, twelve in the **BERKONOMICS** series, *"Extending the Runway"* originally published by Aspatore Press (and now by the BERKUS Press), and co-author of *"Better than Money!"* All are books for emerging growth technology company executives. Dave serves as Board Member of the San Gabriel Valley Council of **Boy Scouts of America**, former Board Member of the **Forum for Corporate Directors**, and is Chairman of the Advisory Board of the technology arm of the **ABL Organization**, a networking organization of CEOs in high tech businesses.

He is often engaged as keynote speaker for events worldwide, speaking on trends in technology and of legal and practical issues of governance for emerging company corporate boards. He tells stories of entrepreneurs who have wildly succeeded or failed, deriving lessons from each for his audience. His TEDx talk, *"Smile at success; Laugh at failure,"* is available on YouTube as are other of segments of his keynotes. His televised *"Berkus Report"* segment of *Eye on Business*, can be found on Time Warner cable and other cable channels nationwide.

To contact Mr. Berkus for speaking engagements or workshops, email dberkus@berkus.com , or phone (626)355-5375. Dave's books are available for purchase from the above website, or the same source from which this book was purchased.

Subscribe to the free weekly email or blog, www.Berkonomics.com**, containing much of the information from Dave's books with lots of comments from readers with their own stories to tell.**

Follow Dave on Twitter (@daveberkus) and Facebook (Dave.Berkus).

Other books by Dave Berkus available directly from *www.berkus.com* or from your favorite bookseller or online store:

EXTENDING THE RUNWAY
Aspatore Press / Thompson West Publications

The five tools board members and executives can use to help their companies succeed. How boards and CEOs should relate to each other for growing the enterprise. Fifty-eight critical questions boards and management should consider in order to assure their mutual alignment.

BASIC BERKONOMICS
Hard cover, soft cover and eBook editions

Volume one of this series. Over one hundred critical insights for entrepreneurs, CEOs and board members covering the life of the company from ignition through liquidity event. Written with basic explanations for terms and methods, as well as insights into planning and measurement for success with small business startups.

BERKONOMICS
Hard cover, soft cover and eBook editions

Volume two of this series. One hundred and one critical insights for entrepreneurs, CEOs and board members covering the life of the company from ignition through liquidity event. Dave tells over fifty stories to illustrate his insights, culled from his experience as entrepreneur and service on over forty corporate and ten non-profit boards.

About the author...

BERKONOMICS WORKBOOK

Companion to BERKONOMICS, this very personal journal contains 101 exercises for the CEO or manager that make each of the insights contained in BERKONOMICS come to life in the form of provocative and actionable questions to be answered right on the pages of the workbook. Once completed, this workbook becomes the manager's personal blueprint for business growth.

ADVANCED BERKONOMICS

Hard cover, soft cover and eBook editions

Volume two of this series. One hundred and one critical insights for entrepreneurs, CEOs and board members covering the life of the company from ignition through liquidity event. More advanced insights into planning and measurement for success with small business startups.

SELLING YOUR BUSINESS!

SMALL BUSINESS SUCCESS SERIES
A Series of eight short and inexpensive books or eBooks

Take all the great material in the BERKONOMICS series and slice it by subject, and you'll have these eight inexpensive, short books about issues that you and your management team needs to focus upon today. Ideal for giving to your entire management group for group discussions and business planning sessions.

BOOKS and eBOOKS IN THIS SERIES:

1. *Starting up!*
2. *Raising Money*
3. *Positioning for Success*
4. *Managing your Workforce*
5. *Protecting your Business*
6. *Growing your Business*
7. *Building Great Boards*
8. *Cashing Out!*

www.ingramcontent.com/pod-product-compliance
Lightning Source LLC
Chambersburg PA
CBHW021923170526
45157CB00005B/2159